MW01042270

The Vet

by Amy Levin

Reading Consultant: Wiley Blevins, M.A.
Phonics/Early Reading Specialist

COMPASS POINT BOOKS

Minneapolis, Minnesota

Follett, Dec.'04, County, #9.75

Compass Point Books
3109 West 50th Street, #115
Minneapolis, MN 55410

Visit Compass Point Books on the Internet at *www.compasspointbooks.com*
or e-mail your request to *custserv@compasspointbooks.com*

Photographs ©: Cover–pg. 12: Capstone Press/Gary Sundermeyer

Editorial Development: Alice Dickstein, Alice Boynton
Photo Researcher: Wanda Winch
Design/Page Production: Silver Editions, Inc.

Library of Congress Cataloging-in-Publication Data
Levin, Amy, 1949-
  The Vet / by Amy Levin.
      p. cm. — (Compass Point phonics readers)
  Summary: Shows a veterinarian at work·in an easy-to-read text that
  incorporates phonics instruction and rebuses.
  Includes bibliographical references (p. 16) and index.
    ISBN 0-7565-0528-3 (hardcover : alk. paper)
  1. Veterinarians—Juvenile literature. 2. Veterinary
medicine—Juvenile literature. 3. Reading—Phonetic method—Juvenile
literature. [1. Veterinarians. 2. Veterinary medicine. 3. Rebuses. 4.
Reading—Phonetic method.] I. Title. II. Series.
  SF756.L48 2003
  636.089—dc21   2003006373

Table of Contents

Dear Parent or Caregiver,

Welcome to Compass Point Phonics Readers, books of information for young children. Each book concentrates on specific phonic sounds and words commonly found in beginning reading materials. Featuring eye-catching photographs, every book explores a single science or social studies concept that is sure to grab a child's interest.

So snuggle up with your child, and let's begin. Start by reading aloud the Mother Goose nursery rhyme on the next page. As you read, stress the words in dark type. These are the words that contain the phonic sounds featured in this book. After several readings, pause before the rhyming words, and let your child chime in.

Now let's read *The Vet*. If your child is a beginning reader, have him or her first read it silently. Then ask your child to read it aloud. For children who are not yet reading, read the book aloud as you run your finger under the words. Ask your child to imitate, or "echo," what he or she has just heard.

Discussing the book's content with your child:
Explain to your child that vets care for pets that are sick or hurt. But vets also see healthy pets that come for checkups so that they can stay healthy. Some vets specialize in treating farm animals or animals in zoos or wildlife parks.

At the back of the book is a fun Hop Scotch game. Your child will take pride in demonstrating his or her mastery of the phonic sounds and the high-frequency words.

Enjoy Compass Point Phonics Readers and watch your child read and learn!

To Market

To market, to market,

To buy a **fat pig,**

Home again, home again,

Jiggety **jig.**

To market, to market,

To buy a **fat hog,**

Home again, home again,

Jiggety **jog.**

To market, to market,

To buy a **fat hen,**

Home again, home again,

Jiggety **jen.**

To market, to market,

To buy a **fat cat,**

Home again, home again,

Jiggety **jat.**

To market, to market,

To buy a **fat bug,**

Home again, home again,

Jiggety **jug.**

Dr. Kim is a vet.
Dr. Kim helps pets.

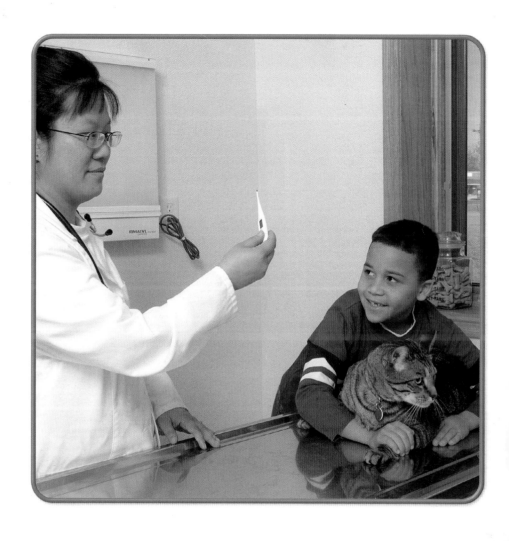

A fat cat is sick.
Dr. Kim will give it pills.

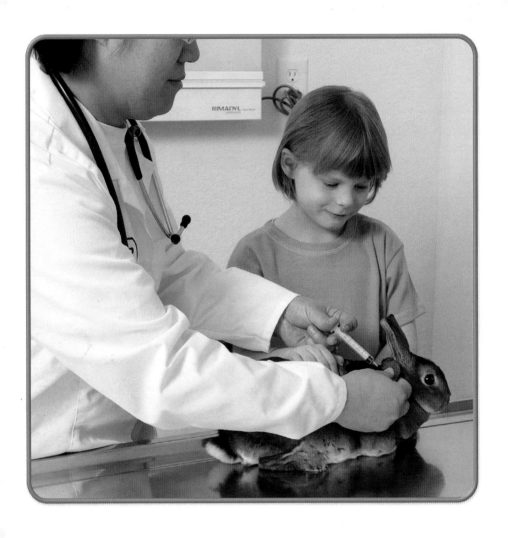

A tan rabbit gets a shot.
The shot will make it well.

A cat has a bad leg.
It gets a cast.

A dog has glass in its paw.
Dr. Kim can help.

This pup is not sick.
Dr. Kim keeps it healthy.

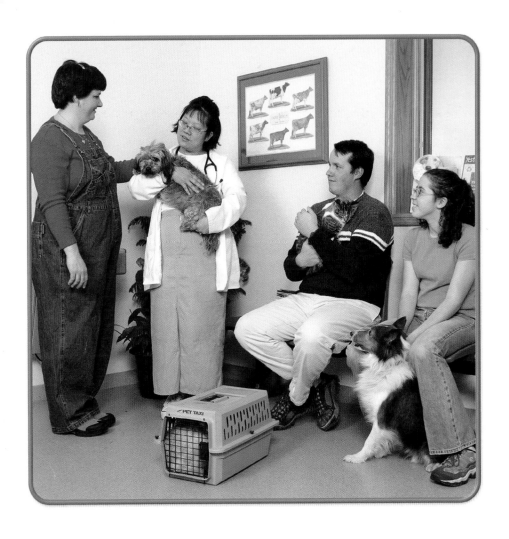

A vet can help your pet.
Stop in and visit.

Word List

Short Vowels

Review of
short *a*
short *e*
short *i*
short *o*
short *u*

s-Blends

cast
stop

High-Frequency

gives
keeps
this
your

Social Studies

healthy
paw
shot

Hop Scotch

You will need:
- 1 penny
- 2 moving pieces, such as nickels or checkers

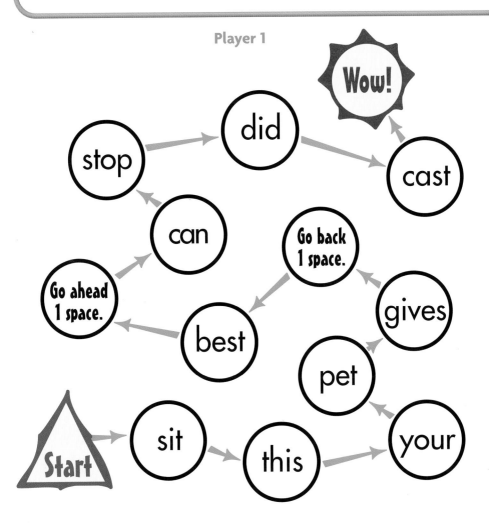

How to Play

- Each player puts a moving piece on his or her Start. Players take turns shaking the penny and dropping it on the table. Heads means move 1 space. Tails means move 2 spaces.
- The player moves and reads the word in the circle. If the child cannot read the word, tell him or her what it is. On the next turn, the child must read the word before moving.
- If a player lands on a circle having special directions, he or she should move accordingly.
- The first player to reach the *Wow!* sign wins the game.

Player 2

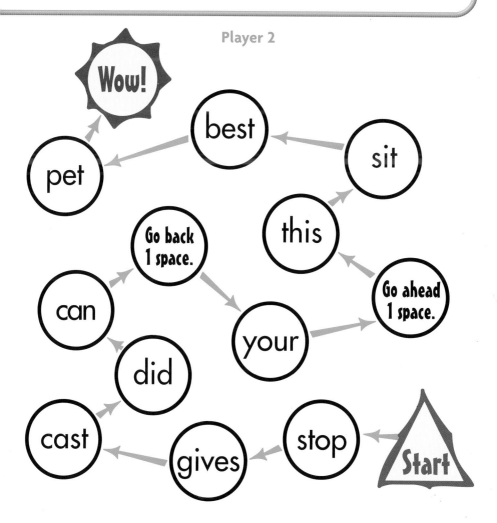

Read More

Blackaby, Susan. *A Cat for You: Caring for Your Cat.* Minneapolis, Minn.: Picture Window Books, 2003.

Frost, Helen. *All About Pets: Dogs.* Mankato, Minn.: Pebble Books, 2001.

Miller, Michaela. *Rabbits.* Des Plaines, Ill.: Heinemann Interactive Library, 1998.

Raatma, Lucia. *Veterinarians.* Community Workers Series. Minneapolis, Minn.: Compass Point Books, 2003.

Schaefer, Lola M. *We Need Veterinarians.* Mankato, Minn.: Pebble Books, 2000.

Index